HOW DO THEY DO THAT?

written by Anne Miranda
illustrated by Tim Egan

Table of Contents	Page

Mc Graw Hill **Macmillan McGraw-Hill**

New York   Farmington

First let's do the math. Hurry up, get your calculator!

For every second of an animated movie, your eye is actually seeing 24 pictures. They flash by so quickly that they appear to be moving.

An animated movie may run for an hour and 15 minutes. (That's 75 minutes.) How many seconds is that? (There are 60 seconds in one minute, so multiply 60 x 75.) If there are 24 pictures per second, how many pictures are there in the movie? (Multiply the number of seconds by 24 frames per second.)

It takes a staggering 108,000 pictures to make a 75-minute animated feature. If you drew 10 pictures a day—even on weekends—it would take you over 29 years to draw 108,000 pictures.

How do these movies ever make it to the theaters? Teamwork! Hundreds of people work on one movie. Watch the list of credits at the end.

Some kinds of animation take less time, for example, clay animation and computer animation. Most animation, however, is still done the "old-fashioned" way.

CEL ANIMATION

In the process called cel animation, each picture is drawn by hand, and then the pictures are filmed. Most cartoons you see Saturday morning on television, as well as those in movies and on videos, are cel animations.

Before animators start drawing, though, they need a story. Even the greatest artist can't make a great film without a story. Choosing a story that will inspire an audience is the first challenge in making an animated film.

That story is written out in a *script*. The script contains the dialogue, or words that each character will say. The script also describes the action in every scene. An animation script is very much like that used in a live-action movie.

After the script is finished, the dialogue is recorded. Those are real actors talking—sometimes popular ones you might have seen in live-action movies. The animation must be timed with the recorded dialogue to look natural on screen.

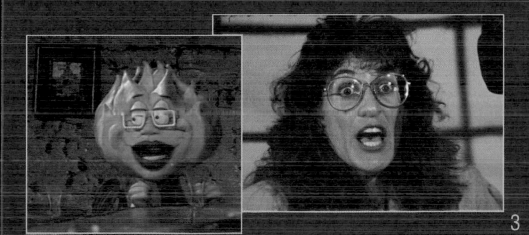

Because so many animators are working together, each scene must be carefully planned. There can be no guesswork once production begins. The movie director must sketch the most important elements of the action. This process is called *storyboarding*. A storyboard is like a blueprint that will help animators plan each scene. The storyboard is kept in a central location so the director and animators can consult it for reference. Animation studios are sometimes located in large lofts, or floors of old warehouses, so that everyone has plenty of room to work.

With the storyboard in place, the animation department goes to work. Their first job is to create the characters. *Characterization* is probably the most challenging task. What will the characters look like? How will they move? How will they act? It is the animator's job to give life to something that doesn't exist. Just think of the cartoon characters you know and love. Don't they seem real to you?

A *lead animator* plays a key role. He or she decides what the characters are going to look like, how they are going to "act" in each scene, and how each scene is going to develop. There are often many lead animators on a movie. Sometimes there is one lead animator for each character.

The lead animator outlines a scene by sketching the main elements of the action, or *keyframes*, with paper and pencil. The keyframes indicate that the character is to go from here to there. Other animators draw the action that connects the keyframes. They provide the movement between "here" and "there." Often these sketches are filmed to check the "look" and timing of a scene.

If the "look" and the timing of the scene are good, a whole team of artists cleans up the drawings and transfers them onto *cels*. A cel is a piece of a clear material known as cellulose acetate. The outlines of the characters are simply inked in first. Sometimes the drawing is photocopied onto the cel. Then each cel is painted. When the cel is complete it will be filmed over a background.

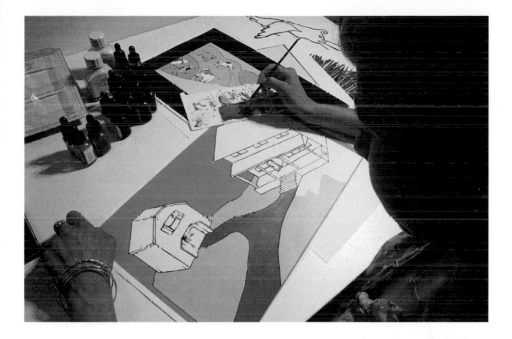

Meanwhile, another team of artists is producing the *background art*. Background art is the setting in which the action takes place. Generally, each scene has a different background. A haunted castle, a shady forest, a living room, a schoolyard, a space station—think how important background art is to the cartoons we watch. Often the background images are more detailed than the cels. A single background may take much more time to prepare than a single cel.

Remember the calculation you did on page 2? It gave you the number of cels in a 75-minute movie. To find the total number of pieces of art generated for an animated movie, you would have to add all the background pictures as well.

Everything that moves or changes within a scene is painted on the cels. The transparent cels are filmed one at a time on top of the background art. Often, if there are several characters in a scene, each is drawn on a different cel. Then the cels are overlapped and photographed together.

When all the cels are filmed and the soundtrack is added, the movie is ready. The individual frames appear on the screen for a fraction of a second. Our brains fill in the gaps between the pictures. We "see" them move even though they don't actually move at all. It's an illusion the magic of animation creates.

Some videocassette players have a single-frame advance. If you have access to one, put your favorite cartoon or movie in and watch it frame by frame. This will give you a sense of how cel animation works. A half second of footage may look like this:

CLAY ANIMATION

Clay animation is another method of bringing objects to life. The characters and often the backgrounds in clay animation are three-dimensional, not flat drawings like cels. Like cel animation, clay animation is used for cartoons, commercials, and sometimes full-length movies.

Clay animators have to fill the same 24 frames per second. But the characters do not have to be drawn again for each frame. Instead, they are made of movable clay. The same figure can be used again and again. After each shot, animators move the figure to the next position. Although clay animation requires careful planning and lots of patience, it does not take as many people to make a clay-animated movie.

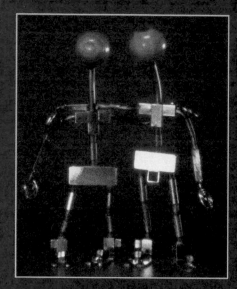

Although we call it clay animation, animated characters are often molded from *plasticine*. Plasticine can be worked easily. It is sturdy and holds its shape once it is molded. Unlike other types of clay, plasticine does not dry out. It can withstand hot lights and will hold up for the length of time it takes to shoot the movie.

Large figures are often made over an *armature*. An armature can be a simple wire frame, like a skeleton which helps the figure keep its shape.

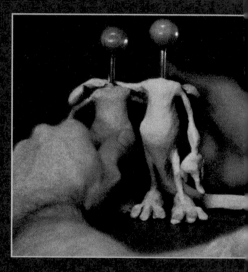

Clay puts more limits on an artist to form a character than pencil and paper. The lines and shapes of a clay character are thicker and less precise. The features of the face cannot be made as fine, and subtle changes of mood are harder to show.

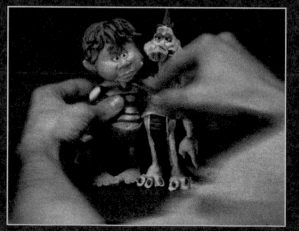

As in cel animation, moving figures are filmed against backgrounds. In some clay animations, the backgrounds are flat, like paintings. In others, the figures move through three-dimensional *sets*. The sets are similar to those in a play. Sets can contain real objects or objects made of clay, or a combination of both.

As in a live–action film, lighting is very important in clay animation. Three-dimensional figures all cast shadows. Lights must be placed so that the shadows fall where the animator wants them. The lights cannot hinder the people working the figures, and shouldn't be bumped or moved during filming.

The characters are made. The sets are ready. The lights are in place. Now the animator is ready to begin filming.

Anything else that moves in the scene has to be changed slightly from frame to frame in order to create movement in the scene. One frame of film is shot. Then the animator moves the character just a bit. Another frame is shot. The animator moves the character again. Hundreds of adjustments are made to shoot each scene.

The animator must time the character's movement precisely. Too great a change from frame to frame creates movement that looks jerky. If the change is too small, characters will look as though they are moving in slow motion. Mistakes are difficult to correct.

When all the scenes are filmed, the film is *edited*. Editing means cutting and pasting strips of film together to create a seamless movie.

COMPUTER ANIMATION

A computer is the animator's latest tool for creating moving images. With computer art, there is no paint, no clay, no lights, no sets, and not even a real camera. Every image in the film exists in the memory of a machine.

Using drawing programs, artists can create pictures that resemble those of cel animation. Computers can also create objects that look three-dimensional. If you watch television, you have probably seen both types of computer animation used in commercials, opening credits for television programs, music videos, and cartoons. There have even been a few full-length films using only computer animation.

Creating a three-dimensional character on a computer is more than pushing buttons. A character may be created from a set of *primitives*. Primitives are three-dimensional shapes such as a cone or a cube that are stored in the computer's memory. The computer can show these from all sides, not just one view. The shapes can be put together to make a figure. It's like having a set of digital building blocks.

Another way to create a figure is to create a *mesh*. A mesh is a computer image of something like a wire frame. It can be given the shape and outline of a figure. When the basic figure is put together, the animator uses computer tools to "cover" it with color and texture. The figure has to be "lit" to create shadows and a three-dimensional look.

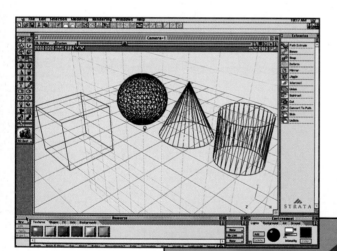

The actual "drawing" of the figure is called *rendering*. Rendering sometimes can be done in *real time*. Real time means that as you give the computer an instruction you can see the results on the spot. Rendering often takes much longer. Once a figure is rendered, it can be stored and then changed as needed to give it movement and character.

Making a character move from place to place can be done in two ways. Either each frame can be assembled by the animator or keyframes can be made by the animator showing a start and an end position. Here is where the computer comes in handy. It can be programmed to calculate how an object gets from "here" to "there" in the required number of frames. Then the computer creates detailed in-between images.

You are probably used to computers working very quickly. The huge amounts of information in animated images, however, take a long time to process. It might take a computer two hours to render a frame of film. Let's go back to our number problem. In a 75-minute movie, there are 108,000 individual frames of film. How many hours would it take the computer to draw them? How many years? Is that more or less than it would take you? Check your answer below.

This is too long to wait! Animators use many computers working together to make a movie. The computers do the work of dozens of artists.

No matter which type of animation is used, the challenge is the same. The goal of any animator is to tell a great story that looks fantastic!

Answer: It would take 216,000 hours. If you have a calculator, divide 216,000 by 24 hours per day, and divide the result again by 365 days per year. It will take about 24 years to make the film.